THE FUNNIEST ARSENAL QUOTES... EVER!

About the author

Gordon Law is a freelance journalist and editor who has previously covered football for the *South London Press*, the *Premier League*, *Virgin Media* and a number of English national newspapers and magazines. He has also written several books on the beautiful game.

Also available to buy

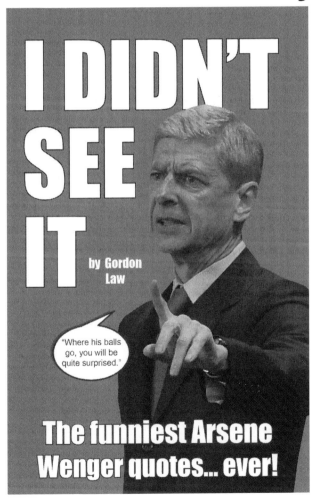

gordonlawauthor@yahoo.com

Printed in the United States of America
ISBN-13: 978-1539793670
ISBN-10: 1539793672

Photos courtesy of: Maxisport/Shutterstock.com and Ramzi Musallam.

Proofreader: Stewart Coggin.

Contents

Introduction

"It took a lot of bottle for Tony Adams to own up to his drink problem" was probably not the best choice of words from Ian Wright, but it was arguably his funniest.

That classic blooper was one of many from the Arsenal striker who is never shy in speaking his mind – and much of it to comic effect.

Wright's former manager Arsene Wenger is another Gunners legend, who to this day, continues to amuse us with a stream of humorous quotes.

His rants, musings on players and confused cliches have entertained, while his war of words with managerial rivals Sir Alex Ferguson and Jose Mourinho have been enthralling.

George Graham also came out with some witty remarks – but it's the observations on him from his old players that are even funnier.

The Arsenal dressing room has been filled with many larger-than-life characters over the years which has led to hilarious sound bites to go with the various title triumphs and cup wins.

Charlie Nicholas, Tony Adams, Charlie George, Ray Parlour and Lee Dixon are some of the players who have shown a wicked sense of humour. And how can we forget the real-life caricature that is Nicklas 'Lord' Bendtner?

You'll find many of their bonkers one-liners and plenty more in this ludicrously funny collection of Gunners quips and quotes. Hope you enjoy!

Gordon Law

THE FUNNIEST ARSENAL QUOTES... EVER!

PLAYER POWER

"The only problem is that he bores the pants off us with his philosophies, his piano lessons, the plays he has been to see, the books he has read."

David Seaman on Tony Adams who was recovering from alcoholism

"He's focused and determined, but also very young. I don't think he even shaves yet."

Arsene Wenger on Jack Wilshere, aged 16

"At Arsenal he told me he'd played in nine World Cups – and he was only 23!"

Ray Parlour on Kanu, who claimed to be 33 but many felt he is older

"[Manuel] Almunia took the criticism and responded with one word – his performance on the pitch."

Arsene Wenger uses five words instead of the one

"Ray is without doubt the funniest player I've ever trained with. It's so important to have players such as Ray involved with the group, for his contribution on the field and spirit off it. I only wish I could understand more of what he says."

Gilles Grimandi on Ray Parlour

"To me, he will always be the Romford Pele."

Marc Overmars on Ray Parlour

"He has that smell to be where he needs to be at the decisive moment. When there is chocolate to take in the box, he is there."

Arsene Wenger on Julio Baptista

"Big Sol never says a word. When we play Spurs and I have a go at him, it's like talking to the deaf and dumb."

Ian Wright on Sol Campbell

"Where his balls go, you will be quite surprised."

Arsene Wenger on Denilson's attributes

"He started reading literature to me and poems and I'd be like, 'Tony we've got a big game tomorrow mate and you're reading me a poem, you're supposed to be kicking the players!"

Ray Parlour on roommate Tony Adams

"The Germans do well economically and we respect that. They are the only ones that make money in Europe. That's why we've chosen a German."

Arsene Wenger explains why German Per Mertesacker was given the job of collecting fines from the Arsenal players

"Martin Keown's movie career is probably over."

Arsene Wenger breaks the bad news after the defender requires stitches following a clash against Wolves

Paul Merson: "Who the f*ck's that?"

Nigel Winterburn: "Bloody hell Merse, it's Nelson Mandela."

"Jens changed his mind but wasn't quick enough to respond to his brain."

Arsene Wenger on a mistake by keeper Jens Lehmann that allowed David Healy to score for Fulham

"As far as I'm concerned, Tony, [Adams] is like the Empire State Building."

Ian Wright

"They are like the lion. He has to catch the animal in the first 200 metres. If he doesn't get there, after he's dead. They are these kind of killers. When they go, it is to kill and after they have to stop."

Arsene Wenger compares Alexis Sanchez [and Jamie Vardy] to the jungle cat

"I can understand everyone apart from Ray Parlour."

Junichi Inamoto

"I think after every match he comes in with a bottle of champagne. He can open a shop now."

Arsene Wenger on Dennis Bergkamp after he was again named man of the match

"We nearly didn't sign him because the letters did not fit on his shirt."

David Dein on the signing of Giovanni van Bronckhorst

"I should invite you sometimes to come into the dressing room and look at the legs of Alex Hleb after a game. You would be amazed."

Arsene Wenger

"He was the man who gave me the courage to wear ripped jeans."

Ashley Cole on Freddie Ljungberg

"I'm amazed how big Patrick Vieira's elbows are – they can reach players 10 yards away."

Arsene Wenger

"Dennis Bergkamp is such a nice man, such a tremendous gentleman, with such a lovely family. It's going to be hard for me to kick him."

Tony Adams on going up against his Gunners teammate on international duty

"If Dennis Bergkamp was in Star Trek, he'd be the best player in whatever solar system they were in."

Ian Wright

"I ran home immediately to my wife in excitement and said, 'I've seen the nearest thing to a Brazilian footballer you'll ever see in our Academy... and he's from Lewisham!'"

David Dein on David Rocastle

"When Ian Wright is going well you must put him in jail to keep him out of the game."

Arsene Wenger

"I don't think it's because of my eyes, my beautiful eyes!"

Arsene Wenger on why Thierry Henry stayed at Arsenal

"He only has to fart during a warm-up and they're singing his name from the rafters."

Ashley Cole on Freddie Ljungberg

"I wish we could use 'Quincy' on his shirt, but they won't let us. I don't know how to pronounce his name – I've tried, but I can't."

Arsene Wenger on Quincy Owusu-Abeyie

THE FUNNIEST ARSENAL QUOTES... EVER!

I DID IT
MY WAY

"When you are a player, you think, 'Me! Me! Me!' When you are a manager, you think 'You! You! You!'"

Arsene Wenger

"I didn't want to play another 300 games with mediocre players and be up against it. I wanted the ball to be up the opposing end so I could get my cigars out at the back."

Tony Adams on playing with star players

"I will never forget my first game for England at the World Cup. It was against Turkey... No, I mean Tunisia."

David Seaman

"I'm 30 now and in five years' time I won't be in this country. That's definite. Italy looks good to me because it would suit my kind of football. Spain is an option."

Sol Campbell before joining... Portsmouth

"I have no regrets, but it is a big surprise to me because he cancelled his contract to go abroad. Have you sold Portsmouth to a foreign country? No."

Arsene Wenger Sol Campbell's decision

"I do not want to sit on the bench, staring. I love playing lots of games."

Nicklas Bendtner

"I hired the ostrich outfit for three years running. I loved it. It had the false legs down the side, you know? A few of the lads started implying that there was something sexual about it."

Charlie Nicholas on the Gunners' annual fancy dress party

"Somehow I got handsomer and sexier every time I progressed up the football ladder. By the time I was in the side I was Robert Redford."

Perry Groves

"No one could ever call me a prima donna."

Ashley Cole

"As for that rumour about me having an erection while I was lying there, that's b*llocks. I never got an erection after scoring a goal."

Charlie George on his famous celebration after scoring the 1971 FA Cup final winner

"I went from being No.1 to No.3 almost overnight, but I tried not to think about it. Maybe I should have left one year earlier, but I had a contract that was too good to refuse."

Jens Lehmann

"Well, I won't be picking it for a while!"

Andy Linighan after scoring the 1993 FA Cup winning goal with a broken nose

"This slice of pizza came flying over my head and hit Fergie in the mush... We all went back in the dressing room and fell about laughing... the United boys did their best not to laugh."

Ashley Cole on 'Pizzagate'

"They couldn't really call me 'Spunky' when the younger fans are around. So they settled on 'H'. It's Cockney rhyming slang: Harry Monk – spunk."

David Seaman

"I can't change that I'm gorgeous."

Olivier Giroud makes a cameo in an anti-homophobia advert

"I don't have a life outside football. When people ask me how I like London, I say, 'Where is London?'."

Arsene Wenger

Reporter: "You're eyes are streaming – are you all right?"

Mel Charles: "I'm OK. I've just got clitorises in my eyes."

The Gunners player suffered from cataracts

"I've wanted to play in pink boots since I was little. The only way anyone can top me now is to play in diamond-encrusted boots."

Nicklas Bendtner

Journalist: "Where would your next move be?"

Nicklas Bendtner: "If I could decide: Real Madrid or Barcelona."

"I didn't watch the England v Argentina match in 1998. I can't remember why not. It may have been past my bedtime."

Theo Walcott

"It's not healthy to be negative. If today I am healthy, I know tomorrow I could die. But if I think like that there's more chance I will die."

Arsene Wenger

"I've never been a goalscorer, only own goals. Good own goals."

Steve Bould

"If I have a lot of adrenaline in my body, that is helpful because I feel less pain."

Jens Lehmann

"For me that must be something special. It is like a boy being told Beyonce is looking for them."

Emmanuel Adebayor admits he is flattered to be pursued by AC Milan

"I liked a fight and I always stood up for myself. That's how I was brought up. Coming from Holloway you learn from the pram to nut people who pick on you."
Charlie George

"I used to think my name was 'Stop the Cross' I heard it so much."
Lee Dixon

"Quite simply, it is true that I can be a pig! It is not a lie to say that. Sometimes, I feel I am in the right even when I'm in the wrong,"
Thierry Henry

"Everyone thought I was lifting up my shirt to kiss the Arsenal badge or wiping away a tear. But it was Patrick and his bloody Vicks."

Ashley Cole revealed he got Patrick Vieira's Vicks in his eye

"If you ask me if I am one of the best strikers in the world, I'd say 'yes' because I believe it."

Nicklas Bendtner

"I am not going to leave. Never. I am staying here for life."

Thierry Henry stays at Arsenal shortly before he leaves for Barcelona

"Everything I do I always feel very confident. Whether it's tennis, badminton, football, whatever. I just go out there and think I can do it and most of the time I can. What I'm good at I don't mind saying because it's not a secret, is it?

Nicklas Bendtner

"I played so badly that even my parents booed me off when I was substituted."

Theo Walcott on playing for England U21s

"There is no chance of me flying and I am not prepared to have any form of counselling."

Dennis Bergkamp, the non-flying Dutchman

"I think I lost my barnet [hair] flicking the ball on for all them years at the near post from Brian Marwood's corners."

Steve Bould

"I want to be top scorer in the Premier League, top scorer at the World Cup and over the next five years I want to be among the best players in the world. Trust me, this will happen."

Nicklas Bendtner

"I'd compare myself to Zinedine Zidane – a humble guy who just happened to be the best."

Nicolas Anelka

THE FUNNIEST ARSENAL QUOTES... EVER!

A FUNNY OLD GAME

"It was very nice for me to play in Ian Wright's testimonial! The occasion surpassed all of my dreams."

Lee Dixon after Ian Wright hogged all the limelight in his testimonial game

"The fans who gave me stick are the ones who still point at aeroplanes."

Ian Wright

"We have all had more fun than this. Have you ever known a colder night?"

Martin Keown after the defeat by Shakhtar Donetsk in Moscow

"At White Hart Lane, the two teams were going down the tunnel and I felt this tugging from behind. As I was about to step on to the pitch with 30,000 people watching, Gazza was trying to pull my shorts down. Luckily, they were tied firmly or I would have made my entrance with my kecks around my ankles."

David Seaman

"The trick was to get in early as possible, hit them hard, give them a good wallop, make them feel as if they'd been in a car crash or hit a brick wall."

Peter Storey

"Once it was lucky Arsenal. Then it was boring Arsenal, but now we've got a real problem because we're in danger of being liked."
Peter Hill-Wood

"It's a bit hard to play like a gentleman with someone closely resembling an enthusiastic member of the mafia swiping his studs down your legs, or kicking you up in the air from behind."
Eddie Hapgood, playing for England in a bad tempered match against Italy at Highbury

"It's impossible for us to match Chelsea's spending power – unless we find oil at Highbury."

Arsene Wenger on Roman Abramovich's riches

"A 0-0 draw in Italy is crap. A 0-0 draw in England can be really interesting."

Ian Wright on Serie A

"Goalkeeping is like extreme sports sometimes – you have to let yourself go."

Jens Lehmann

"When the captain said there was a problem at the back I thought he meant me and Steve Bould."

Tony Adams after an Arsenal flight was delayed

"Roman Abramovich has parked his Russian tank in our front garden and is firing £50 notes at us."

David Dein

"When I called Coventry supporters a bunch of w*nkers, it was the best 15 grand I ever spent."

Ian Wright

"Our objective is to keep Arsenal English, but with a lot of foreign players."

Peter Hill-Wood

"I haven't seen [Ronaldinho's] winner yet. It's not that I'm avoiding it, just that my little girl has been watching Teletubbies all the time."

David Seaman on the chipped free-kick that sent England out of the World Cup

"[Frank] Lampard is a specialist in insulting people very badly."

Jens Lehmann

"It took me a long time to understand that the song they sing about me was not trying to bully me. People explained to me that it was more an expression of love."

Per Mertesacker on the song, 'We've got a big f*cking German'

Q: "Where would you like your ashes scattered?"

A: "Half at Highbury, half at White Hart Lane."

Ian Wright

"Dennis Bergkamp told me the Dutch always thought of the English as strong but stupid."

Tony Adams

"That will always be a memory for everyone else I suppose. The winner's medal and scoring the goal are my memories."

Steve Morrow reflects on being dropped by Tony Adams and breaking his collar bone after the 1993 League Cup final replay

"When you're dealing with someone who has only a pair of underpants on and you take them off, he has nothing left. He is naked. You're better off trying to find him a pair of trousers to complement him rather than change him."

Arsene Wenger doesn't want to stifle a player's flair

"I have flown economy and haven't had a problem with it."

Peter Hill-Wood on putting the players in the cheap seats for a pre-season tour

"I don't know where they are. I think the guys who come and clean the house take them!"

Arsene Wenger seems a bit careless with his old FA Cup medals

"I am so sorry. I have been unable to sleep after what happened... I promise I will replace this unhappy situation with happy things."

Jose Antonio Reyes on his own goal in a League Cup semi against Middlesbrough

"Kenny Dalglish came on at the same time as me and everyone expected him to win it for Liverpool. But here I was, a ginger-haired no-body, setting up the winning goal for Arsenal."

Perry Groves on the 1987 League Cup final win over the Reds

Q: "What it was like to win the FA Cup?"

A: "It's f*cking excellent."

Freddie Ljungberg

"People come up to you and remind you of your mistakes, but it helps being 6ft 4in and 15½ stone."

David Seaman

THE FUNNIEST ARSENAL QUOTES... EVER!

BEST OF ENEMIES

"Call me old fashioned, but we don't need his money and we don't want his sort. They only see an opportunity to make money. They know sweet FA about our football and we don't want these types involved."

Peter Hill-Wood after reported interest in the club by US businessman Stan Kroenke

"Bruce Rioch labelled me Charlie Big Potatoes."

Ian Wright after handing in a transfer request in 1996

"I have to accept that there are people who don't have a clue about football."

Jens Lehmann on criticism he's facing

"When I heard the figure of £55k I nearly swerved off the road. I yelled down the phone, 'He's taking the p*ss, Jonathan [Barnett, his agent].' I was so incensed, I was trembling with anger."

Ashley Cole on finding out Arsenal would not pay him £60,000 a week

"I wouldn't play for Arsenal again, even for £200,000 a week."

Ashley Cole after talks with Chelsea

"He is my favourite enemy... I loved every aspect of his game."

Patrick Vieira on Roy Keane

"He's always complaining, whingeing. To me he's deceitful as well as being a nasty piece of work... He's a great player, I can't deny it... but for me the man is a cheat and a thief. He is a coward who is sneaky in the way he goes about fouling other players. Everyone thinks he's a nice guy but in fact he's a son of a bitch."

Patrick Vieira on Ruud van Nistlerooy

"To those who say it's a step back, I say b*llocks."

Ian Wright on being picked for England at the age of 34

"I made two mistakes at the beginning of the season. But I saw Manuel Almunia making mistakes as well, so sometimes you don't know what the thoughts of the coach are."
Jens Lehmann on Manuel Almunia

"To be sitting on the bench behind somebody who only started to play when he was 30 is not funny."
The goalkeeper takes another swipe at his Gunners rival...

"He does not have my class."
...and another

"I think Arsene's a great manager. The trouble is that if you ever make a valid point about him and the club, it's like criticising the Pope. Everybody gets up in arms."

Frank McLintock

"First thing we taught him was: 'Tottenham are sh*t'."

Ian Wright helps Patrick Vieira learn English

"I always dreamed of winning the league at White Hart Lane. So I left and joined Arsenal."

Sol Campbell

"My worst fears were confirmed as Thierry and I sat in the centre circle after the final whistle. His name was sung from the rooftops, while my contribution was recognised by a deafening silence. It was like I was the invisible man."

Ashley Cole

"I don't respect Alan [Hansen] because he has never put his head on the block [as a manager]. For me to do punditry in the early days would have felt very hypocritical."

Tony Adams

THE FUNNIEST ARSENAL QUOTES... EVER!

"I felt his attitude suggested he was doing me a favour, like I was a 17-year-old trainee."

Ashley Cole on David Dein

"You're a big-nosed French tw*t."

Paul Merson to David Ginola during a Cup Winners' Cup semi-final against Paris Saint-Germain just before he scored

"I'd have killed the German b*stard!"

Robert Pires after being substituted in the Champions League final for tactical reasons after Jens Lehmann was sent off

"My coach [Arsene Wenger] confirmed to me my impression that he uses a different measuring stick to evaluate [Manuel] Almunia. For me, this was a huge disappointment. That has forced me to think about my situation. I have to ask myself what is still realistic and possible for me at Arsenal? When Wenger says something like that, it's going to be difficult for me to get back in here. It's very frustrating. When I see the performances on the field, I get angry and I have to clench my fist in my pocket."

Jens Lehmann

"He takes himself far too seriously and thinks he is very important. I don't like it when someone glorifies them self."

Jens Lehmann on Germany goalkeeping rival Oliver Kahn

"I do not have a 24-year-old girlfriend. I have another life altogether."

Lehmann has a dig at Kahn's love life

"He looks like a nice boy but on the pitch it is not always fair behaviour."

Arsene Wenger on Ruud van Nistelrooy

"I didn't score as many as I hoped, but it was nice that I always scored against Tottenham."

Charlie Nicholas

"I have found Alan Sugar to be one of the least charming people I have ever come across."

Peter Hill-Wood

"He tries it on in every match and somehow gets away with his butter wouldn't melt in his mouth act. I think he actually spends as much time on the floor, rolling around, as he does scoring goals. I find it hard to respect someone like him."

Ashley Cole on Ruud van Nistlerooy

"My relationship with Lehmann is the same as ever – we don't really have one."

Manuel Almunia on Jens Lehmann

"[David] Dein bought me for £500,000 and sold me for 44 times as much, so he has made a huge profit. And he still tried to block things. This man only thinks about money."

Nicolas Anelka

"Sometimes it does happen – a child can fight with his father and they are still friends."

Emmanuel Adebayor on his on-field argument with Nicklas Bendtner against Tottenham

"People have perceptions on you and they're based on portrayals written by guys who've had five minutes with you. Why get worked up about it?"

Sol Campbell on the media

"If you end up at Man City, I really believe you are a player who thinks only about money."

Gael Clichy, speaking just months before he signs for... City

"The boss told us to put up with his 'little ways' because he scored lots of goals for us, but at times it was so hard."

Theo Walcott on Robin van Persie

"I just wish the record was going to someone else. I don't have a very high opinion of Ian Wright."

Joan Bastin, widow of striker Cliff Bastin, on Ian Wright going for Arsenal's all-time scoring record

"I tried to watch the Tottenham match on television in my hotel yesterday, but I fell asleep."

Arsene Wenger fires a shot at the rivals

"I've never been so insulted by anyone in football as this little upstart puppy."

Denis Hill-Wood on Brian Clough

"This guy should never play again. The answer is 'he is usually not that type of guy'. It's like a guy who kills one time in his life – it's enough, you have a dead person. It is absolutely horrendous. If you watch the tackle again you can't say to me this guy has played the ball. It's a joke. Not acceptable. It goes along with the idea that to stop Arsenal you have to kick Arsenal and we knew that thing would happen one day."

Arsene Wenger after Birmingham's Martin Taylor broke Eduardo's leg

"I'm no longer part of Arsenal. To hell with the English people."

Nicolas Anelka

"[Alex] Ferguson's out of order. He has lost all sense of reality. He is going out looking for a confrontation, then asking the person he is confronting to apologise. He's pushed the cork in a bit far this time and lost a lot of credibility by saying what he said."

Arsene Wenger responds to Sir Alex Ferguson who accused Wenger of confronting him with raised hands following United's 2-0 win. And also failing to apologise for his players' bad behaviour in the tunnel which led to pizza and soup being thrown at Ferguson

"If there is an apology, it must be coming by horseback."

Arsene Wenger after Sir Alex Ferguson claimed Arsenal "turned games into battles"

"I'm ready to take the blame for all the problems of English football if that is what he wants."

Arsene Wenger responds to Sir Alex Ferguson who questioned Arsenal's lack of British players

"Alex Ferguson's weakness is that he doesn't think he has any."

Arsene Wenger

"He's out of order, disconnected with reality and disrespectful. When you give success to stupid people, it makes them more stupid sometimes."

Arsene Wenger threatens to take legal action against Jose Mourinho for calling him a voyeur

"I know we live in a world where we have only winners and losers, but once a sport encourages teams who refuse to take the initiative, the sport is in danger."

Arsene Wenger takes a swipe at Jose Mourinho's negative style of football

"If you would like to compare every manager you give each one the same amount of resources and say, 'You have that for five years'. After five years you see who has done the most."

Arsene Wenger has a pop at Chelsea boss Jose Mourinho

"It is fear to fail."

Arsene Wenger after being asked why some managers [Mourinho] were playing down their title chances

THE FUNNIEST ARSENAL QUOTES... EVER!

SAY THAT AGAIN?

"In France we have a saying, 'When you fill a vase with water, it only takes one drop to make the water overflow'."

Emmanuel Petit on being targeted by referees

"The goal that Charlton scored has aroused Arsenal."

George Graham

"I don't see things the way my parents do. They can look at a tree and see something amazing, whereas I just see a tree."

Robin van Persie on his artistic parents

"Modern society wants less pain, to suffer less and be treated better in every aspect. Pain has to disappear, whether you go to the dentist or go to work."

Arsene Wenger

"Outside of quality we had other qualities."

Bertie Mee

"I've been consistent in patches this season."

Theo Walcott

"He's given us unbelievable belief."

Paul Merson on Arsene Wenger

"I was in the car with my dad and brother. A kid was walking down the road with a 'Walcott 32' shirt on. I put the window down and said 'I've got a shirt like that too'!"
Theo Walcott

"It sounds ridiculous but I always put my watch into the right pocket of my trousers. If anybody wants to nick it, they'll know where to look now I suppose."
Steve Bould

"I never doubted, but when you don't win the game you wonder if you are right."
Arsene Wenger, that sounds like a doubt

Say That Again?

"On the pitch I appear to be fragile but week by week I am ripening."

Cesc Fabregas, aged 19

"If you are living like an animal, what is the point of living? What makes daily life interesting is that we try to transform it to something that is close to art."

Arsene Wenger

"I'm five short – not that I'm counting."

Ian Wright on breaking the Arsenal goalscoring record

"It's like a child who is used to having ice cream whenever he wants. When it doesn't come when he asks, he tends to get confused and nervous."

Arsene Wenger uses a dessert analogy to describe losing top spot in the league

"un flwyddyn heddiw."

Aaron Ramsey's tweet in Welsh with a photo from his wedding. Translated, it means: "One year [ago] today"

"I like to be a tiger roaming the jungle or an eagle soaring the skies."

Sol Campbell

Say That Again?

"At the end of the day, the Arsenal fans demand that we put 11 players on the pitch."

Don Howe

"Left alone with our own heads on, we can be pretty mental."

Tony Adams

"He is like a block of ice, untouched by excitement."

Herbert Chapman on Cliff Bastin

"I am supposed to take the bullets and absorb them. Like a bear. A polar bear."

Arsene Wenger on criticism from the supporters

"[Johan] Cruyff was almost as good as myself."

Charlie George

"It will make me go quicker."

Anders Limpar on shaving his body hair

"I want to explode with Arsenal."

Sylvain Wiltord

Say That Again?

"Like the Tibetans I have learned to understand myself, even if you never fully can."
Emmanuel Petit

"The biggest things in life have been achieved by people who, at the start, we would have judged crazy. And yet if they had not had these crazy ideas the world would have been more stupid."
Arsene Wenger

"Playing another London side could be an omen, but I don't believe in omens."
George Graham

THE FUNNIEST ARSENAL QUOTES... EVER!

MANAGING JUST FINE

"I used to enjoy movies and going to the theatre, but I don't have much time for that now. My way of relaxing is to watch a football match on television at home. I suppose for most men that might cause trouble, but at least I have the excuse that it's my job!"

Arsene Wenger

"I never thought of taking him off. It's nothing to worry about, it gives the face character."

George Graham on Andy Linighan after the defender scored the 1993 FA Cup winning goal with a broken nose

"It was like Japan turning to France for a sumo manager."

Arsene Wenger reflects on his appointment as a French manager in English football

"I feel like Marje Proops sometimes, having to deal with you lot."

Bruce Rioch in agony aunt mode with his players

Reporter: "Why did you take Jack Wilshere off?"

Wenger: "It was 9.25, past his bedtime."

Wilshere was then aged just 16

"I admit I am single-minded. I think all of the great football managers have been single minded."

George Graham

"In my job, you expect to suffer. That's why when I go to hell one day, it will be less painful for me than you, because I'm used to suffering."

Arsene Wenger

"Shave that off. You will not play for Arsenal until you do."

Bertie Mee to a bearded Charlie George

"Am I suggesting there were a lot of bad tackles? Leave me alone with that, for f*ck's sake."

Arsene Wenger is furious with Birmingham's physical style

"I think John Lukic is one of the best three goalkeepers in the country. I just think David Seaman is the best."

George Graham

"We still have not found a machine who can measure the intensity of love. We would all buy it."

Arsene Wenger after Theo Walcott commits to the Gunners

"What is unbelievable is that, I am in a position where people reproach me for making a profit. The people who lose money – nobody says a word. Reproach the people who lose money. I do business by managing in a safe way and a healthy way, and on top of that you reproach me for making money. It looks like we are in a business where the desired quality is to lose money."

Arsene Wenger in sarcastic mode

"What's it like being in Bethlehem, the place where Christmas began? I suppose it was like seeing [Ian] Wright at Arsenal."

Bruce Rioch

"What happened to that Ryan Wilson you used to rave about?"

George Graham to Sir Alex Ferguson – the surname of Giggs' dad

"I sometimes say to footballers' agents: 'The difference between you and me is that if there were no more money in football tomorrow, I'd still be here, but not you."

Arsene Wenger

"As long as no one scored, it was always going to be close."

Stating the obvious from Arsene Wenger

"You live in a marginal world as a manager. I know three places in London: my house, Highbury and the training ground [in Hertfordshire].

Arsene Wenger

"It was a surprise, but a very pleasant one. I had not planned to become a football club manager."

Gunners physio Bertie Mee is appointed the new manager

"I am on earth to try to win games."

Wenger states his life mission

"One of the things I discovered in Japan was from watching sumo wrestling. At the end you can never tell who has won the fight, and who has lost, because they do not show their emotion because it could embarrass the loser. It is unbelievable. That is why I try to teach my team politeness. It is only here in England that everybody pokes their tongue out when they win."

Arsene Wenger on a technique picked up from his time with Grampus Eight in Japan

THE FUNNIEST ARSENAL QUOTES... EVER!

CALL THE MANAGER

"Once in Norway I went up to him, put my arm around him and asked him how he was, just so I could put a lemon on his shoulder without him noticing. It was a silly joke and gave the lads a good laugh, but George was not happy about it. He was even less happy when Niall Quinn once put a condom there."

Tony Adams on George Graham

"The new manager has put me on grilled fish, grilled broccoli, grilled everything. Yuk!"

Ian Wright on Arsene Wenger

"I remember George [Graham]. He was a bit of a poseur at first, a bit lazy when he played up front, the last one you could imagine going into management. Different now. He has poseurs for breakfast."

Frank McLintock

"George Graham was telling Lee Chapman that if footballers looked after themselves there was no reason they could not play until 35. Then he looked over to me and said, 'Well, maybe not you, Quinny'."

Niall Quinn

"The biggest bollocking I got in six years of playing for Arsene was when we lost a game and he came in and said, 'I cannot stand for this. This is not acceptable'."

Tony Adams

"If there was ever a player I felt definitely would not have what it took to be a manager it was George Graham. Running a nightclub? Yes. A football club? Absolutely not.

Don Howe

"He loved a 1-0 win, he really did."

Steve Bould on George Graham

"George Graham's regime was like living in Iraq under Saddam [Hussein]. He was disgusting. You would turn up for training and he would call [one player] into his 'room', though it wasn't a room because everyone could hear what he was saying. Then he would say, 'I've sold you to Leeds'. So the player replies, 'I don't want to join Leeds'. Graham then says, 'Well, you just have to pack your bag and leave'. What a swine. I have never seen a guy like that [player]. Tears running down his cheeks. He'd been at Arsenal since he was 16."

Anders Limpar

"George [Graham] will be happy with a draw – I know how ambitious and positive he is."

Terry Neill

"He arrived unnoticed at the training ground. A meeting was called, the players filed in and in front of us stood this tall, slightly built man who gave no impression whatsoever of being a football manager."

Lee Dixon on Arsene Wenger

"I don't think I'm big-mouthed enough to be a manager."

Robert Pires

"At the moment I'm just swallowing it all as part of the humiliation but I think – and this is aimed at my dear manager – one shouldn't humiliate players for too long."

Jens Lehmann on being left out of the side by Arsene Wenger

"I played with him for six years. I've met him a few times. The more I got to know him the less I know him. I haven't a clue how that man thinks, how he works. He's difficult to fathom."

Tony Adams

"He's a cold, pompous man."

Charlie George on Bertie Mee

"One of the first things Arsene Wenger did at Arsenal was to make sure players couldn't get pay-per-view in hotels. If players are exciting themselves quite a few times then it's going to affect their physical condition."

Tony Adams

"It is new to me to have someone checking your diet and giving you all kinds of tips – what to eat, when to eat, how to chew, when to eat chicken, when to eat fish, when to eat meat. You would think that is easy."

Giovanni van Bronckhorst on Arsene Wenger

"Once, we were in a hotel, and Arsene Wenger went up to the dessert trolley whilst everybody is sitting down as normal. He's got the spatula out with his apple pie, and as he has turned around, the pie fell off his plate. And you talk about he doesn't see a lot – but he didn't see his apple pie fall off his plate I'm telling you! So he's walked through all of the players, with everybody smiling, watching and waiting. He finally sits down at his table, gets his spoon out, looks down, and says, 'Where's my apple pie?'"

Ray Parlour on Arsene Wenger who literally didn't see it!

"The fact he personally contacted me and made so much effort to recruit me, it has seduced me."

Bacary Sagna is in love with Arsene Wenger

"I have to be honest and say that I felt [England manager] Bobby Robson was a bit bumbling at times. When I first turned up for training, he called me Paul Adams."

Tony Adams

"He told you how to dress. He told you how to do your hair."

Eddie Hapgood on Herbert Chapman

"I told him in no uncertain terms to go and f*ck himself."

Charlie George to Don Revie after being substituted by the England manager

"Every time he speaks to me I have this image of him showing me his pips on his uniform."

Sol Campbell on George Graham

"I've got to play for a Frenchman? You have to be joking."

Tony Adams recalls his reaction to Arsene Wenger's appointment

"When Arsene came to Arsenal he took complete control of our diets. We were allowed no salt, no fat, and no sugar, in the end you wanted to play a team like Millwall so that someone would throw a banana at you just so you could have something to eat."

Ian Wright on Arsene Wenger

"Arsene Wenger has put me down a few times. The annoying thing is, he does it intelligently and I hate that. Sometimes I want to punch him on the nose."

Tony Adams

"I drove home thinking, 'You tight Scots b*stard, it's not your money'."

Perry Groves on George Graham who refused to increase his wages

"When Arsene first came to Arsenal, we called him Clouseau and then Windows because of those boffin's glasses."

Tony Adams

"When he spoke I tended to drift off."

Charlie George on Bertie Mee

THE FUNNIEST ARSENAL QUOTES... EVER!

WOMAN TROUBLE

"After having sex the night before [a match], I lose all feelings in my feet. I'm totally empty. I can't control the ball any more. Instead I watch erotic movies the night before. That doesn't affect my power."

Freddie Ljungberg

"It is very easy in England to find a girl who wants to be with you for the wrong reasons."

Wojciech Szczesny

"Next time I'll learn to dive maybe, but I'm not a woman."

Thierry Henry after defeat to Barcelona in the Champions League final

"I apologise to my wife, family and friends and my manager, teammates and Arsenal fans. I now have to fight for my family and for my club and obtain their forgiveness. Nothing else matters at the moment."

Olivier Giroud apologises for taking a female back to the team hotel

"A football team is like a beautiful woman. When you do not tell her so, she forgets she is beautiful."

Arsene Wenger

"It's hard to be passionate twice a week."

George Graham

"At 9am on Saturday, he [Ray Parlour] called me. I told him I was in bed... He said, 'Kal, I'm leaving'. I said, 'What, Arsenal?' And he said, No, you'. I said, 'Let's talk about this – tell me why you're leaving'. He said cool, 'I can't talk now. I'm at the hotel and I've got a game this afternoon and have to concentrate."

Karen Parlour, ex-wife of Ray, after being awarded a large divorce settlement

"I'm really proud of my medals. No one can take them away from me. Not even my ex."

Ray Parlour

"[Married players] have more emotional stability unless they are married to a nightmare."

Arsene Wenger

"I don't have a girlfriend for the moment but I'm a heterosexual. These rumours are completely false."

Freddie Ljungberg

"Arsenal Ladies would do really well [against Tottenham's men]. I'm sure they would get a point."

Cesc Fabregas

"She was attractive, 20 or 21 and a virgin. In that part of the world that's like finding a penny black, I can tell you."

Perry Groves on his wife Mandy

"It was as if I'd spent ages making love to the most beautiful woman in the world only to be kicked out of bed five minutes before the climax."

Peter Storey on fears about being axed for the FA Cup final in 1971

"I didn't get too many women running after me. It was their f*cking husbands who'd be after me."

Charlie George

"My mother always talked a lot and she told Arsenal's chief scout that I'd be OK as long as I was given lots of chips. So the chief scout said, 'We'll call him Chippy'. In that one second, I was given a nickname which lasted throughout my eight years at Arsenal."

Liam Brady joining Arsenal as a teenager

"You're Arsenal players and you're having your picture taken with a c*nt like that! It's just not on!"

George Graham to Michael Thomas and Ian Wright, who had a photo with actress Antonia de Sancha. She was famous for having an affair with MP David Mellor

"It's like you wanting to marry Miss World and she doesn't want you. I can try to help you but if she does not want to marry you what can I do?"

Arsene Wenger after Jose Antonio Reyes said he wanted to leave Arsenal

"I love England, one reason being the magnificent breasts of English girls. Women are ultimately all that matters in life. Everything that we do is for them. We seek riches, power and glory, all in order to please them."

Emmanuel Petit

"I usually don't have sex. Not on the same day. I say no thanks. I guess that, mentally, I want to keep the feeling in my feet and that's why. I think the feeling sort of disappears out of your feet if you have sex before. I have tried before and my feet felt like concrete when you are supposed to kick the ball."

Freddie Ljungberg

"Young footballers should be married, and looking after themselves in the evenings to ensure they're fit and healthy."

Bruce Rioch

THE FUNNIEST ARSENAL QUOTES... EVER!

LIFESTYLE CHOICE

"I'd never seen a footballer wearing pyjamas before! Normally a player will have nothing on. And Dennis comes out in full pyjamas! That stands out more than anything else. It was so lovely. Pyjamas!! It was so sweet."

Ian Wright on Dennis Bergkamp

"But for the record... I don't smoke."

Jack Wilshere tweets

"I think in England you eat too much sugar and meat and not enough vegetables."

Arsene Wenger

"We get the BBC in Holland so I know about Ceefax. I call up page 301 and I'm shocked. The first two lines are in huge letters: 'Bergkamp joins Arsenal'. For the first time it hits me: "Woah! What's going on here?" I'm in this big country. I'm in London. I'm in this huge strange city where they drive on the left and… I'm on teletext. Me!"

Dennis Bergkamp is delighted to have made it on Teletext

"I didn't know the English were good at swimming. I have been in this country for 12 years and I haven't seen a swimming pool."

Arsene Wenger

"They do everything for you. We're treated like babies, really. So much so that there are some players, not necessarily at this club, who wouldn't know how to check in at an airport."

Lee Dixon

"It took a lot of bottle for Tony Adams to own up to his drink problem."

Ian Wright

"I don't watch cricket. How can you like a game that requires you to take four days off work to follow a Test?"

Thierry Henry

"What's really dreadful is the diet in Britain. The whole day you drink tea with milk and coffee with milk and cakes. If you had a fantasy world of what you shouldn't eat in sport, it's what you eat here."

Arsene Wenger was surprised at how English players ate when he arrived in 1996

"I remember a book by Dr Robert Haas. It was called 'Eat To Win' and we had that in 1987, long before Arsene ever came to these shores. OK, we were drinking 20 pints of lager as well, but we were still eating pasta!"

Tony Adams

"When I first started getting called Champagne Charlie. I couldn't afford champagne! I was on the shandy, if I was lucky."

Charlie Nicholas

"I know that if I go to the club to play, sooner or later I will end up trying to smash the [golf] ball with my foot."

Thierry Henry doesn't like golf

"I moisturise daily with Nivea and I regularly use Nivea body lotion."

Freddie Ljungberg

"Could you get us all a pair of those Calvin Klein's? We want the special ones like yours, the ones with a sock down the front. We've seen you in the shower and you're really not that big."

Dennis Bergkamp on Freddie Ljungberg's modelling

"I like to sit around the house and watch TV programmes – but I really like playing football on my Xbox in my boxer shorts."

Cesc Fabregas

"I drank nine bottles of wine a day."

Kenny Sansom

"I was obviously worried. My body is my livelihood and I was desperate to find out if I was OK. So I took off all my clothes, even my pants, picked up a wing mirror that had come off the car and checked myself over, front and back."

Nicklas Bendtner on stripping naked next to the wreckage of his brand-new £160,000 Aston Martin that he crashed

"I can't remember the last two championships because I was drinking, so I'll savour every moment of this."

Tony Adams on winning the Premier League title in 1998

"People are talking about me more than they talk about EastEnders."

Thierry Henry on transfer speculation

"It's about the drunken parties that go on for days – the orgies and the fabulous money."

Peter Storey

"My secret is adapting to the country I am in. Here I eat roast beef and Yorkshire pudding. There are people who visit different countries and don't adapt. It is a must."

Arsene Wenger

"I like the comfort of jeans and the elegance of a suit. But above all, I love the sensuality and sexuality that emanates from leather. It multiplies one's sensations tenfold."

Emmanuel Petit

"People reckoned I spent all my time in Stringfellow's but I never went there that much. I preferred Tramp."

Charlie Nicholas

"He joined Arsenal a teetotaller and left a serious drinker."

Paul Merson on Perry Groves

"When you play your wife at tennis, you can love her to death but you still want to beat her."

Arsene Wenger

"In my time players had short hair, wore long shorts and played in hob-nail boots. Now they have long hair, short shorts and play in slippers."

Jack Crayston

"I define myself as an Epicurean. I take great pleasure in eating. I'm a salad specialist and I do a good gratin dauphinois at home. And a little tiramisu I learned from granny Giroud."

Olivier Giroud

"We went straight to the pub and the French lads went to the coffee shop. I'll always remember Steve Bould going to the bar and ordering 35 pints for five of us. After we left, we spotted all the French lads in the coffee shop, sitting around smoking. I thought, 'How are we going to win the league this year? We're all drunk and they're all smoking'. We ended up winning the double."

Ray Parlour

"I don't drink alcohol, it destroys people. If you put the wrong fuel in a car it won't go very far."

Arsene Wenger

"Seriously, I was the only player at Ajax who used to have fried eggs for breakfast everyday. It's one of my superstitions. If I don't have a fried breakfast in the morning, I won't play or train well."

Marc Overmars

"There is definitely a price to pay. The biggest thing I miss because of football is that I really, really love to go on a skiing holiday but as long as I have my career, I can't do that because of the risk of being injured."

Nicklas Bendtner

"What's so great about reality? My reality stank. I was ready for a bender."

Tony Adams

"Sometimes on a day off I go to the Krispy Kreme doughnut shop. When we play at home, I go there after the game and it's like a doughnut party. Everyone is eating doughnuts inside their cars – it's like a disco!"

Cesc Fabregas

"Everything in England is shut at 5pm, there is nothing to do, nowhere to go. I just got bored."

Jose Antonio Reyes

Lifestyle Choice

"It is wrong to compare my salary to the salary of businessmen. Compare it to movie actors instead."

Nicklas Bendtner

"Yes I like chips! But I try not to abuse it because I have a diet – I have to prepare like a player."

Arsene Wenger reveals a guilty pleasure

"Crime levels are really high in London. I would not feel comfortable about leaving my wife and children alone at home."

Jens Lehmann

THE FUNNIEST ARSENAL QUOTES... EVER!

REFFING HELL

"Frankly, I did not see what happened."

Arsene Wenger's now famous sound bite began after his second game in charge. Coventry keeper Steve Ogrizovic had to be taken off injured after a malicious tackle from Ian Wright who was lucky not to be red carded

"All referees are incompetent. I can't think of a single one doing a decent job."

Ian Wright

"Sometimes, privately, I say, 'The referee was crap today,' but not publicly."

Arsene Wenger

"Are the rules you can go first for the man when the ball is in the air and everybody decides it's not a foul, or do we make it a judo party and maybe everybody will be happy?"

Arsene Wenger is unhappy with a challenge

"It's getting to the stage where we hate referees and they dislike us."

Kenny Sansom

"We got the usual penalty for Manchester United when they are in a difficult position."

Arsene Wenger slams Mike Riley's decision to award United a spot-kick

"The referee was booking so many people I thought he was filling in his lottery numbers."
Ian Wright

"The referee made a difference. All credit to him, he scored a good second goal for them. I was happy for him. He deserves a good mention."
Arséne Wenger was not pleased with Borussia Dortmund's controversial penalty in a 2-1 defeat

"It's a great profession being a referee. They are never wrong."
Arsene Wenger

"I don't know if the referee was wearing a Barcelona shirt because they kicked me all over the place. If the referee did not want us to win, he should have said so from the off."

Thierry Henry

"It is a great gesture by Fowler and I would like to give him an award of fair play. But if he got that I would also have to give the referee an award for stupidity."

Arsene Wenger on Robbie Fowler who asked ref Gerald Ashby to retract a penalty

"The official today was a muppet."

Ian Wright

THE FUNNIEST ARSENAL QUOTES... EVER!

Printed in Great Britain
by Amazon

33830157R00077